W9-BTL-701

Counting in the Desert 1-2-3

Aaron R. Murray

Enslow Elementary

an imprint of

Enslow Publishers, Inc.

40 Industrial Road
Box 398
Berkeley Heights, NJ 07922
USA

http://www.enslow.com

EAST CHICAGO PUBLIC LIBRARY

EAST CHICAGO, INDIANA

H.H. 8523088

Enslow Elementary, an imprint of Enslow Publishers, Inc.
Enslow Elementary® is a registered trademark of Enslow Publishers, Inc.

Copyright © 2013 by Enslow Publishers, Inc.

All rights reserved.

No part of this book may be reproduced by any means
without the written permission of the publisher.

Library of Congress Cataloging-in-Publication Data

Murray, Aaron R.
  Counting in the desert 1-2-3 / Aaron Murray.
    p. cm. — (All about counting in the biomes)
  Includes index.
  Summary: "Introduces pre-readers to simple concepts about the desert using short sentences and repetition of
words"—Provided by publisher.
  ISBN 978-0-7660-4051-9
  1. Deserts—Juvenile literature. 2. Counting—Juvenile literature. I. Title.
  GB612.M87 2012
  551.41'5—dc23
                           2011037459
Future editions:
Paperback ISBN 978-1-4644-0061-2
ePUB ISBN 978-1-4645-0968-1
PDF ISBN 978-1-4646-0968-8

Printed in the United States of America
032012 Lake Book Manufacturing, Inc., Melrose Park, IL
10 9 8 7 6 5 4 3 2 1

To Our Readers: We have done our best to make sure all Internet Addresses in this book were active and
appropriate when we went to press. However, the author and the publisher have no control over and assume no
liability for the material available on those Internet sites or on other Web sites they may link to. Any comments
or suggestions can be sent by e-mail to comments@enslow.com or to the address on the back cover.

♻ Enslow Publishers, Inc., is committed to printing our books on recycled paper. The paper in every book
contains 10% to 30% post-consumer waste (PCW). The cover board on the outside of each book contains
100% PCW. Our goal is to do our part to help young people and the environment too!

Photo Credits: iStockphoto.com: © Dario Egidi, p. 16, © idizimage, p. 12; Shutterstock.com, pp. 1, 3, 4, 6, 8,
10, 14, 18, 20, 22.

Cover Photo: Shutterstock.com

Note to Parents and Teachers

Help pre-readers get a jump start on reading. These lively stories introduce simple concepts with repetition
of words and short simple sentences. Photos and illustrations fill the pages with color and effectively
enhance the text. Free Educator Guides are available for this series at www.enslow.com. Search for the
All About Counting in the Biomes series name.

Contents

E
M981cd

Words to Know 3

Let's Count! 5

Read More..................... 24

Web Sites 24

Index 24

Words to Know

lizard   scorpion   meerkat

Let's count!

1

One lizard

Two birds

Three scorpions

Four sand dunes

Five kangaroos

Six meerkats

Seven camels

Eight spider legs

Nine cactus fruits

10

Ten cactus arms

Read More

Anderson, Sheila. *What Can Live in a Desert?* Minneapolis, Minn.: Lerner Classroom, 2010.

Auch, Alison. *Life in the Desert.* Mankato, Minn.: Capstone Press, 2011.

Ward, Jennifer, T. J. Marsh, and Kenneth J. Spengler. *Way Out in the Desert.* Lanham, Md.: Cooper Square, 2002.

Web Sites

Kids Do Ecology. *World Biomes*
<http://kids.nceas.ucsb.edu/biomes/desert.html>

Missouri Botanical Garden. *Biomes of the World*
<http://www.mbgnet.net/sets/desert/>

National Geographic Kids. *Desert Landscapes*
<http://kids.nationalgeographic.com/kids/photos/gallery/desert-landscapes/>

Index

bird, 7

cactus, 21, 23

camel, 17

fruit, 21

kangaroo, 13

lizard, 5

meerkat, 15

sand dune, 11

scorpion, 9

spider, 19

Guided Reading Level: A
Guided Reading Leveling System is based on the guidelines recommended by Fountas and Pinnell.

Word Count: 24